The 1910s

Britain in Pictures

The **1910s**
Britain in Pictures

PA Photos

AMMONITE
PRESS

First Published 2008 by
Ammonite Press
an imprint of AE Publications Ltd,
166 High Street, Lewes, East Sussex BN7 1XU

Text copyright Ammonite Press
Images copyright PA Photos
Copyright in the work Ammonite Press

ISBN 978-1-906672-07-2

British Cataloguing in Publication Data. A catalogue
record of this book is available from the British Library.

Editor: Paul Richardson
Picture research: PA Photos
Design: Gravemaker + Scott

Colour reproduction by GMC Reprographics
Printed by Colorprint, China

Page 2: The Coronation
procession passes down
Fleet Street.
22nd June, 1911

Page 5: Civilians and
soldiers of the Royal Army
Medical Corps distributing
refreshments to British
wounded in France.
July, 1916

Page 6: Miss Nora Willis,
the postwoman at Epsom,
with a uniformed postman.
August, 1916

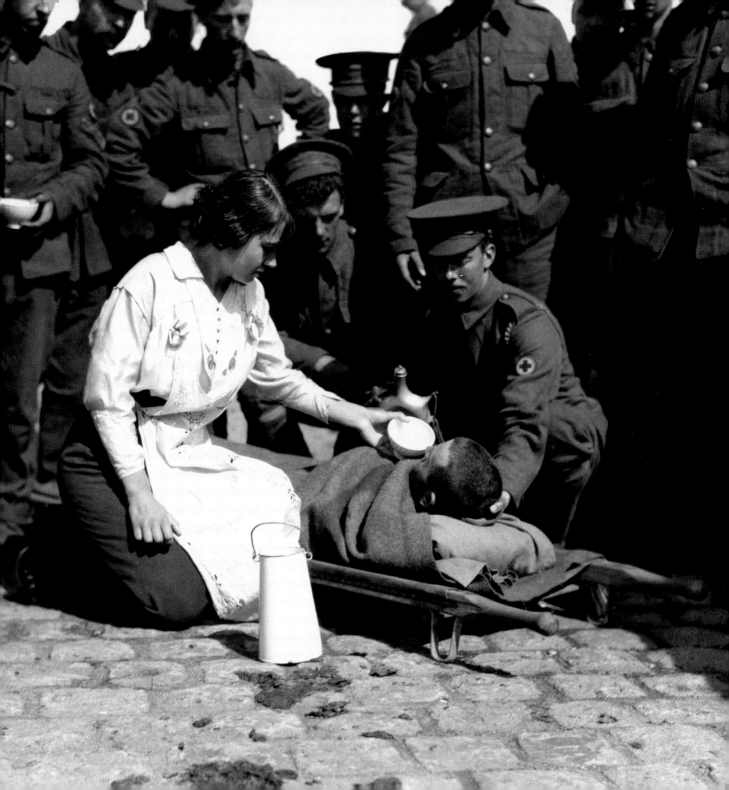

Introduction

The archives of PA Photos yield a unique insight into Britain's recent past. Thanks to the science of photography we can view the 20th Century more accurately than any that came before, but it is thanks to news photography, and in particular the great news agency that is The Press Association, that we are able now to witness the events that made up life in Britain, not so long ago.

It is easy, looking back, to imagine a past neatly partitioned into clearly defined periods and dominated by landmarks: wars, political upheaval and economic trends. But the archive tells a different story: alongside the major events that constitute formal history are found the smaller things that had equal – if not greater – significance for ordinary people at the time. And while the photographers were working for that moment's news rather than posterity, the camera is an undiscriminating eye that records everything in its view: to modern eyes it is often the backgrounds of these pictures, not their intended subjects, that provide the greatest fascination. Likewise it is revealed that Britain does not pass neatly from one period to another.

The decade between 1st January, 1910 and the 31st December, 1919 encompasses a time of deep change in British society. Naturally the Great War – not, of course, the 'War To End All Wars' as was thought, but an apocalyptic episode nonetheless – dominates those years, and is considered to be responsible for the end of the servant culture in Britain. But was it? Even before the War tore a generation of young men from the nation, leaving those who were spared to question the old order, we see conflict between ordinary Britons and their masters. A new industrial unrest was seen on a large scale in the strikes at the beginning of the decade. Women were prepared to die in their struggle to achieve suffrage. In Ireland an armed uprising, surely the most overt statement of dissatisfaction possible, took place.

It is little wonder that those in power watched events in Russia unfold and its Royal family – closely related to Britain's own – overthrown and executed. War or no war, it seems, social upheaval was inevitable.

Suffragettes gathering in
protest outside Queen's Hall,
London.
1910

The **1910s** Britain in Pictures

Captain Robert Falcon Scott RN and Lieutenant Evans of the ill-fated British expedition to Antarctica. Beaten to the South Pole by the Norwegians under Amundsen, Scott and his men perished on the return journey to base camp.
1910

A Zeppelin airship
entering its hangar on
Lake Constance near
Friedrichshafen.
1910

Suffragette activists driving
a bus to demand the vote.
1910

The young Queen Mary
(Princess Mary of Teck)
wife of King George V.
1910

Women workers at
Shorts aeroplane factory,
Shellbeach, on the Isle
of Sheppey.
1910

The Duke of Connaught,
Queen Victoria's son,
with Sir Philip Crampton
Smyley, the Governor
of Sierra Leone.
1910

British Labour leader
and politician Keir Hardie
addresses a public meeting
in Trafalgar Square.
1910

A face in the crowd, George Bernard Shaw (centre, beard), Irish dramatist and critic, at a public meeting in Trafalgar Square. He was an active socialist and Fabian, his progressive ideas informed much of his work.
1910

The Prince of Wales (L, later the Duke of Windsor) and Prince Albert (later King George VI) check the target during shooting practice in the grounds of Balmoral.
1910

Lord Morley passes a horse-
drawn Hansom cab parked
in a London street.
1910

The Honourable Charles
Stewart Rolls, aviator and co
founder of Rolls Royce, with
an early type of triplane at
Shellbeach, where he was
later killed in a plane crash.
1910

A group of Boy Scouts listen intently to their Scout Leader as he instructs them in the art of taking a compass bearing.
1910

A night scene at the Indian
'stand'; a Mughal-style
palace complete with lake, at
the Franco-British Exhibition,
White City, London.
1910

A couple seated on a sea bathing hut at a British seaside resort. The huts were towed into the sea to spare the occupants the indignity of making their way down the beach in their bathing costumes.
1910

Mr and Mrs David Lloyd
George with Winston
Churchill and Mr Clarke.
1910

Two members of the Captain
Scott Antarctica party
– Dr Simpson and Lt Evans.
1910

The Duke and Duchess
of Beaufort at Richmond
Horse Show.
1910

Royal Coach at the state
opening of Parliament.
1910

Queen Alexandra with
her pet dogs aboard
the Royal Yacht during
a visit to Cowes.
1910

Prince Henry & Prince
George receive military
instruction from a member of
a Scottish Regiment.
1910

Mr Moore Brabazon. The first Briton to fly a circular mile in Britain in a British machine, made by Shorts.
1910

The throne, with the Stone of
Scone, Westminster Abbey.
1910

Legendary tenor Enrico
Caruso at home.
1910

Jack Hobbs and
Tom Hayward of
Surrey Cricket Club.
1910

Winston Churchill and his
wife Clementine leaving
Whitechapel Labour
Exchange.
1910

Parliamentary Committee of the Trade Union Congress preparing for the annual meeting in Nottingham.
1910

A radium miner has a
break and smokes his pipe.
Cornwall.
1910

A Suffragette in prison
dress.
1910

Christabel Pankhurst,
Elizabeth Wolstenholme
Elmy, Mrs Mordant
and Jessie Kelly at the
Euston Road Suffragette
procession.
1910

Ludvic Lazarus Zamenhof
(R), an ophthalmologist,
philologist and the inventor
of Esperanto.
1910

Keir Hardie, first Leader
of the Labour Party.
March, 1910

The marriage at Penshurst in
Kent of Mr Hohler and Miss
Laline Astell, daughter of
Lady de Lisle and Dudley by
her first marriage.
9th April, 1910

Newcastle United's FA Cup
winning side.
28th April, 1910

King George V (nearest camera) and Kaiser Wilhelm II of Germany ride in the funeral procession of King Edward VII.
20th May, 1910

Facing page: The funeral cortege of King Edward VII arrives at Windsor, Berkshire, for the King's burial.
20th May, 1910

Captain Scott's ship the
'Terra Nova', before he set
sail on his ill-fated expedition
to the South Pole.
June, 1910

Mr Macintosh, the Duke
of Fife's piper. Braemar
Gathering.
June, 1910

Scouts during a visit to the
Houses of Parliament.
June, 1910

Surrey County Cricket team.
June, 1910

A scene at the Derby,
Epsom.
4th June, 1910

The consecration of
Westminster Cathedral.
28th June, 1910

Wimbledon Ladies' Singles
Final – Dora Boothby
v Dorothea Lambert
Chambers.
July, 1910

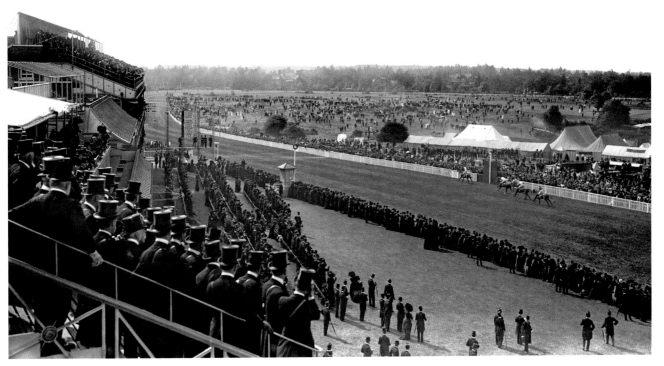

Finish of the Ascot Gold Cup.
8th July, 1910

Two young women enjoy
a day at the seaside. Hove,
Sussex.
August, 1910

Firefloat 'Beta' patrolling
the Thames.
August, 1910

Tossing the caber at
the Braemar Gathering.
September, 1910

Dr Hawley Crippen with Ethel Le Neve, his alleged accomplice, during their trial for murder. Crippen was hanged in Pentonville Prison, London, after being convicted of murdering his wife and hiding her remains in the cellar of his London home in 1910. The couple tried to escape to Canada but were caught after Henry Kendall, the captain of the SS Montrose, recognised Crippen and alerted Scotland Yard.

30th September, 1910

The Seddon Biplane, designed by Lt. J W Seddon R.N. and A G Hackett. Nicknamed 'The Mayfly', the six-seater tandem biplane was the world's largest aeroplane at that time. It was tested at Dunstall Park, Wolverhampton, but failed and was later broken up without ever leaving the ground.
October, 1910

Music hall star, 'Coster Comedian' Gus Elen distributes toys at Christmas to children of Balham district.
December, 1910

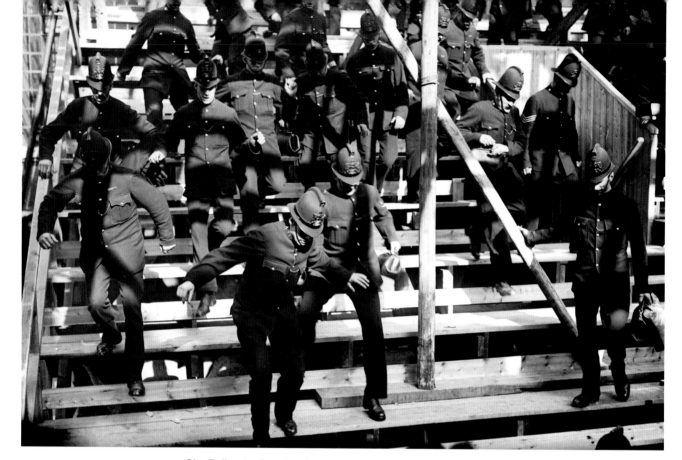

City Police testing stands
before the Coronation.
1911

An early cost-cutting exercise. A camel is put to economic use mowing the lawns at Regents Park Zoo.
1911

Captain Robert Falcon
Scott writing at a table in his
quarters (known as his 'den')
at the British base camp in
Antarctica.
1911

Police and troops escorting
a convoy past a strike
meeting in Liverpool.
1911

Escapologist Harry Houdini.
1911

King George V unveils the memorial to his Grandmother, Queen Victoria, outside Buckingham Palace, London.
1911

Italian radio pioneer
Guglielmo Marconi,
who developed wireless
telegraphy and successfully
transmitted signals across
the Atlantic.
1911

The birthplace of MP John Burns in Simpson Street (now Blean St) in South Lambeth, London. The house was demolished in 1938.

1911

Old Waterloo Bridge.
1911

Police dog pioneer Major Richardson and his dog.
1911

Deadman's Dock, London.
1911

The Prince of Wales
with W G Grace.
1911

York Minster.
1911

Comedienne Miss Louie
Frear, at Eel Pie Island.
1911

Male and female workers
measuring and pinning
the King's coronation train
with ermine.
1911

A new cycle ambulance
for a racecourse.
1911

Bransby Williams as Fagin,
from Oliver Twist.
1911

The Old Curiosity Shop,
Portugal Street, London.
1911

'Titanic' First Officer
William McMaster Murdoch.
Portrayed as a cowardly
murderer in the 1997 movie,
he is seen by historians as a
hero of the disaster.
1911

The Prince of Wales
(second L), later King
Edward VIII, Prince Albert
(second R) later King
George VI and their
tutor Henry Hansell (C),
in Cornwall.
1911

The Marquis of Zetland at
the opening meet of the
Zetland Hunt.
1911

Police frog-marching
a prisoner in Liverpool.
1911

Guardsmen take aim during the siege at 100 Sidney Street, Houndsditch, East London. Guardsmen, police and artillery fought with anarchists besieged in a terraced house. The house caught fire and burned to the ground after Home Secretary Winston Churchill refused to allow the Fire Brigade to intervene.

Winston Churchill
(L, in top hat) during
the siege of Sidney Street in
Houndsditch, East London.
3rd January, 1911

England Team, Rugby Union
– England v France.
28th January, 1911

Water jump at
The Grand National.
21st March, 1911

King George V (C) and
Queen Mary (third R) on
board the P&O vessel
'Medina', manned for the
occasion by the Royal Navy,
en route for India.
April, 1911

Gipsy children running
beside the Royal carriage
during King George V's visit
to Epsom races.
20th May, 1911

A royal garden party at
Buckingham Palace.
1911

French actress Sarah
Bernhardt in 'Theodora'
at the Coliseum Theatre.
June, 1911

Crowds on Ludgate Hill after
the Coronation Drive of King
George V and Queen Mary.
22nd June, 1911

Facing page: The scene
inside Westminster Abbey
during the Coronations
of King George V and
Queen Mary.
22nd June, 1911

The Grand Stand at Royal
Ascot.
23rd June, 1911

Queen Mary with King George V and the Prince of Wales (future King Edward VIII) at the Investiture of the Prince of Wales at Caernarfon.
13th July, 1911

Scottish lasses at their
annual task of cleaning
and packing herrings at the
Suffolk port of Lowestoft.
Scots women traditionally
travelled to ports around
Britain's coast cleaning
and packing seasonal fish
catches.
October, 1911

The England team that
toured Australia.
November, 1911

Queen Mary in her
Coronation Robes. Delhi
Durbar, India. The Durbar,
a state event set up by the
Moguls, was adopted by the
British Raj as a ceremony of
loyalty to the British Crown.
King George V and Queen
Mary were the only reigning
monarchs to visit India
during British rule.
December, 1911

A tiger shoot during
the Delhi Durbar, India.
December, 1911

The new Emperor and Empress of India, King George V and Queen Mary, view their subjects from a balcony during the Delhi Durbar of December 1911. The King announced the founding of New Delhi to replace Calcutta as the capital of British India.

12th December, 1911

The Transatlantic Liner 'Lusitania' moored in the Mersey, Christmas 1911. Her sinking by the German U-Boat U-20 12 miles off the coast of Ireland in 1915, and subsequent loss of life among American passengers, is thought to have influenced the United States to enter the First World War on the Allied side.
25th December, 1911

David Lloyd George arrives at the Houses of Parliament on Budget Day.
1912

The 'unsinkable' four-funnelled ship the 'SS Titanic'. Part of the White Star Line, Titanic sank off Newfoundland on her maiden voyage to the USA after striking an iceberg in April 1912, 1513 people lost their lives.

1912

Captain Robert Falcon Scott
RN (C, wearing balaclava)
and members of the ill-
fated British expedition to
Antarctica.
1912

Meares and Oates in the
stable during their expedition
with Captain Scott to the
South Pole.
1912

Facing page: Snow Hill station closed due to the coal strike over the introduction of a minimum wage for pit-workers. The strike ran from 26th February to 11th April.
1912

England Cricket Captain C B Fry.
1912

Miners race their pet
whippets during the coal
strike in Northumberland. A
row of coal trucks stands idle
in the background.
1912

A strike meeting at Tower Hill in London during the Great Transport Strike.
1912

A view of Nelson's Column from the top of the Duke of York's Column.
1912

Facing page: A fire and rescue in Fleet Street.
1912

Anna Pavlova dancing
with Laurent Novikoff.
1912

Golfer, Mrs Wilcock.
1912

An AA emergency
motorcyclist uses an
Automobile Association
roadside telephone box on
Epsom Road in Surrey.
1912

Conservative Party leader
Andrew Bonar Law speaking
at Blenheim Palace.
1912

A trackless tram; an
early trolley bus, with a
conventional tram on the
East Ham Tramways.
1912

Young tin plate workers
in Swansea.
1912

Children playing in Drury
Lane playground, London.
4th January, 1912

A coal cutting machine
at work.
February, 1912

Girl hockey players
in Hyde Park.
March, 1912

Queen Mary meets men in
the stocks at Shakespeare's
England, Earl's Court.
March, 1912

The new Quadriga
(a chariot and four horses),
on the Wellington Arch at
Constitution Hill, Hyde Park
corner, London.
April, 1912

The scene inside Oceanic
House, London, after the
news of the 'Titanic' disaster.
15th April, 1912

The triumphant Barnsley
team pose with the FA
Cup at Oakwell after their
1-0 replay victory over West
Bromwich Albion.
25th April, 1912

Prominent Conservative, opponent of Irish home-rule and lawyer, F E Smith (later Lord Birkenhead) speaking at Blenheim Palace.
June, 1912

A pontoon bridge section
being rowed into position.
June, 1912

A Welsh choir
at Crystal Palace.
June, 1912

Sir George Frampton's statue of Peter Pan in Kensington Gardens.
June, 1912

The new Admiralty Arch, designed by Sir Aston Webb, constructed by John Mowlem & Co.
June, 1912

Cheridah de Beauvoir Stocks, the second British woman to win a pilots' licence, and Pierre Verrier at the first ladies' aviation meeting at Hendon. They won the 'Speed Handicap with Passenger'.
6th July, 1912

The gold medal winning
Great Britain Women's
4x100m Freestyle team
at the Stockholm Olympic
Games.
8th July, 1912

Great Britain's Arnold
Jackson beats USA's Abel
Kiviat and Norman Taber to
the gold in the Stockholm
Olympic Games – Men's
1500m Final.
10th July, 1912

Aston Villa goalkeeper
Sam Hardy.
26th October, 1912

Street hawkers at Christmas.
December, 1912

Future Prime Minister David
Lloyd George addresses
a meeting at Sutton on
Ashfield.
1913

Comedian George Robey
tees off.
1913

The Crystal Palace, South
East London. The mainly
glass structure was built to
house the Great Exhibition
of 1851.
1913

Tea magnate and yachtsman
Sir Thomas Lipton seated at
his writing table.
1913

St. Catherine's Church, Hatcham, burnt down by suffragettes.
1913

City of London
mounted police.
1913

Marble Arch Corner
from Bayswater Road.
1913

Millicent Fawcett, who
founded the National Union
of Women's Suffrage, at the
Suffragette Pilgrimage in
Hyde Park.
1913

The beach at Margate, Kent.
1913

The Marylebone Cricket
Club (MCC) team leaves
for South Africa on the deck
of the Saxon.
1913

Prime Minister Herbert
Henry Asquith.
1913

Unloading tobacco at
Victoria Docks, London.
1913

A view of the 'Ivory Floor' where elephant tusks, boar tusks, narwhale horns, rhinoceros horns and sometimes mammoth tusks are ranged in incredible profusion. It was said that many were old treasures of chiefs, stored perhaps for centuries in remote African villages.
1913

Raw rubber being prepared
for sale.
1913

Suffragettes at a mass
meeting in the Royal
Albert Hall.
1913

Detectives watch Emmeline
Pankhurst's house in
Manchester Square, London.
1913

A delegation with a bouquet to be presented to Queen Amelie of Portugal, at the Fairyland Bazaar Fete at the Horticultural Hall, London.
1913

Margaret and David Lloyd George at the base of Moel Hebog, North Wales.
1913

Facing page: Tea time at Ranleagh.
1913

Dr Hertz opens the new
synagogue in Brixton, London.
1913

Ye Old Cogers' Discussion Hall at Salisbury Court. The Society of Cogers was a free speech society, established in 1755. Still running today, it is the oldest debating society in the world.

1913

The Daily Mail newspaper
in operation in room 55 at
Carmelite House, Fleet Street.
1913

Boulter's Lock on the
Thames on Ascot Sunday.
1913

A group of Oldham mill girls in traditional costume wait with Lancashire policemen for a visit from King George V.
1913

Police raid the offices of the W.S.P.U. (suffragettes) in Kingsway, London.
1913

The Tea Pavilion in Kew Gardens, burnt down by suffragettes.
20th February, 1913

Judging the Brace class.
Old English Sheepdog
Show, Aldridges, St Martin's
Lane, London.
6th March, 1913

England's F E Oakeley tries
to break down the wing, with
support from team-mates.
England v Scotland, Five
Nations Championship.
15th March, 1913

FA Cup Final, the victorious
Aston Villa team (Aston Villa
v Sunderland).
20th April, 1913

A general view of the huge
crowd at Stamford Bridge
for the Amateur Cup Final,
South Bank v Oxford City.
26th April, 1913

Two monarchs. King George V and Kaiser Wilhelm II leave the Potsdam Palace to attend a review staged by the Kaiser.
26th May, 1913

The Royal Pavilion, Brighton.
June, 1913

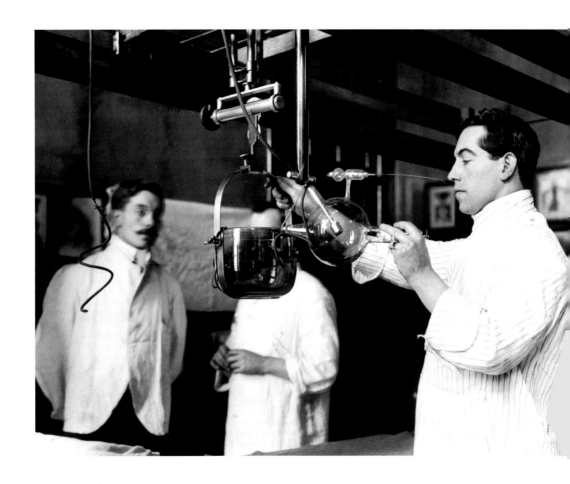

An X-ray machine in operation.
June, 1913

The view north over Tower
Bridge into the City of
London.
June, 1913

Jockey Herbert Jones is carried away on a stretcher after fracturing his skull when Emily Davison threw herself in front of his horse Anmer during the Epsom Derby.
4th June, 1913

Mrs Margot Asquith watches
Trooping the Colour from the
wall of Downing Street.
13th June, 1913

The funeral procession of
suffragette Ascot protester
Emily Davison.
14th June, 1913

Stonehenge, Wiltshire. The sarsen stones are buttressed with timber to prevent their collapse.
August, 1913

Volunteers prepare for action at a meeting in Larne. Protestant Ulstermen, armed with Boer War-era British Army equipment, were organised to resist Home Rule for Ireland 'by any means necessary'.
August, 1913

King George V's racing
yacht 'Britannia' in full sail.
August, 1913

Incoming American
champion Francis Ouimet
(plus fours) looks on as
Harold Hilton drives.
10th October, 1913

Hetty Green, the world's richest woman. Reputedly a miser, in earlier life she refused to have her young son's broken leg treated when they were recognized at the hospital: he later lost it to gangrene. She also refused treatment for a painful hernia, when her personal fortune ran to several-hundred million dollars, because the treatment would cost $150.

21st November, 1913

The Prince of Wales (middle
row, second R) drills with the
Officer Training Corps.
1914

Scott's ship 'Discovery'.
1914

Andrew Carnegie, US
steel manufacturer and
philanthropist, posing in
the entrance of his Scottish
home.
1914

Royal Navy Volunteer Reserves
reporting for war duty.
1914

The 3rd Dragoon Guards
leave for Egypt.
1914

Derby day.
1914

Facing page: The Pearly
King of Hoxton accompanied
by a Pearly Prince and
a Pearly Princess on the
course at the Derby.
1914

The British fleet anchored
in Torbay, Devon.
1914

Workmen, in Fairfields
Shipyard, Govan, Glasgow,
cheering King George V and
Queen Mary on a Royal visit.
1914

Sir Ernest Rutherford, Langworth Professor of Physics at Manchester University, and 'atom counting' apparatus.
1914

Facing page: A woman swimmer enjoys the sea.
1914

Winston Churchill mounted
for polo in Madrid.
1914

Ex Prime Minister Arthur Balfour making a speech at the Unionists' Garden Party at Penshanger, Hertford.
1914

A steam lorry load of Naval
reserve kitbags.
1914

Lord and Lady Baden-Powell and local dignitaries at the Great Scout Rally Manchester.

1914

A French officer of artillery controlling the fire of a battery of Soixante-Quinze field guns (75s). The armoured observation post is a ladder mounted on the ammunition caisson or limber. Le Roi de la Guerre, as the 75 was known, could fire 25 to 30 75mm rounds per minute.
1914

Field Marshal Lord Roberts
VC in the full ceremonial
dress of the Irish Guards,
wearing shamrock for St.
Patrick's Day.
17th March, 1914

England Team. Five Nations
Championship – England v
Scotland.
21st March, 1914

Lloyd George going to the
Commons to present the
Budget.
10th April, 1914

FA Cup Final at the Crystal
Palace. Burnley v Liverpool.
25th April, 1914

New recruits drilling on the
terrace of Crystal Palace,
then requisitioned as a naval
training establishment.
June, 1914

The Prince of Wales leaves
in full marching kit for active
service as a Grenadier
Guards recruit.
June, 1914

Trooping the Colour.
13th June, 1914

Messrs. Ross (L) and Collinson (R) engaged in a bare knuckle bout.
1st August, 1914

Facing page: With so many men called into service, women were employed to do 'men's' work such as ticket collecting at Victoria.
4th September, 1914

French peasant women tend
the graves of British soldiers.
1st October, 1914

David Lloyd George.
20th October, 1914

Ruins of the Bennett house in Scarborough, damaged by shells fired by the German battle cruisers SMS Derfflinger and SMS Von Der Tann, when a force of German warships under Admiral von Hipper shelled Hartlepool. 17 people died in the attack, all civilians, the youngest being 14 months old.
16th December, 1914

Winston Churchill speaking
at the Enfield Lock Munitions
Works. Mrs Churchill is
seated on the left.
1915

French troops in their trench wearing an early type of gas mask.
1915

Poster produced with the aim of boosting enlistment in Ireland. Campaigners for home rule saw the war in a rather different light.
1915

Queen Alexandra and Sir Dighton Probyn VC, her household Comptroller, visit blind workers making piano parts.
1915

A British soldier checks
through his equipment.
These waist length fur coats
of many colours were issued
to some allied troops as
winter gear.
1915

An Army Chaplain helping a
German prisoner.
3rd January, 1915

Ancient and modern: London
cabs at Charing Cross.
February, 1915

Sheffield United, FA Cup
winners 1914-15. Sheffield
United v Chelsea.
May, 1915

Anti-German demonstrators
break Schoenfeld's window
in Crisp Street, Poplar,
London.
13th May, 1915

Painting grey horses brown
for camouflage.
June, 1915

Rudyard Kipling (R) appeals for recruits. Next to Kipling is the Mayor of Southport in volunteer uniform and Naval Surgeon Avarne, who went down with the Goliath and swam for four miles before being rescued. Kipling's only son Jack was recorded missing believed killed at the battle of Loos in September 1915.

June, 1915

Lord Kitchener making his
great recruiting speech at
the Guildhall, London.
9th July, 1915

A woman employed by
Cowley's Dairy sells milk
from a churn in the streets of
Brighton, Sussex.
August, 1915

British and Indian Army soldiers shifting a field gun over a 'bund'. The Indian Expeditionary Force advanced along the River Tigris towards Baghdad during Summer 1915 as part of the war against the Ottoman Turks. Part of the expedition, 6th Poona Div., later came to grief at the siege of Kut-Al-Amara surrendering to the Turks in April 1916.

August, 1915

British soldiers from the
Dorset Regiment negotiate
hiring a 'ballam' from an
Arab boatman.
August, 1915

Wounded British soldiers
being carried on to a hospital
ship at Basra.
August, 1915

Shackleton's icebound ship 'The Endurance'. After the ice pressure was released, she sank between the ice floes: the floes came together again, shearing off the masts and top deck and thrusting the ship below the ice into the waters of the Weddel Sea.

27th October, 1915

A British soldier pays his respects at the grave of a comrade near Cape Helles, where the Gallipoli landings took place.
November, 1915

On Christmas Day, hostilities ceased in favour of football. Officers and men of the 26th Divisional Train, A.S.C. enjoy a game at Salonika, Greece.
25th December, 1915

British soldiers of the Royal
Artillery hitch a ride on a
lorry carrying a pile of kit
bags at a French port.
1916

British 'Tommies' of various English and Scottish regiments in France on their way to the front. Note the age of the Scottish soldier, front rank, second from left.
1916

Canadian soldiers enjoying a midday meal outside their sandbagged position amid the mud following storms on the Western Front. A wartime censor has erased the men's shoulder badges.
1916

Welsh National Eisteddfod,
Aberystwyth.
1916

Boy 1st Class, John Travers Cornwell VC, boy hero of the Battle of Jutland, remained at his post throughout the battle after being mortally wounded. He was 16 years old.

1916

The Royal family including King George V, Queen Mary and Princess Mary (L) during a visit to Aldershot with Field Marshal Sir Douglas Haig, Commander in Chief of forces on the Western Front.
1916

Key Irish rebel, Countess Markievicz, seen through a cellar window. Imprisoned in Liberty Hall for her part in the Easter Uprising, on having her sentence of death commuted to life imprisonment she commented; "I wish your lot had the decency to shoot me."
1916

Women employed on Government work, felling trees in Kenstoke Woods near Weston-Super-Mare.
1916

Mrs Page driving one
of the trams at Weston-
Super-Mare.
1916

British West Indian troops in physical training at Kingston, Jamaica.
1916

Women ambulance drivers
changing a tyre on a
Siddeley-Deasy ambulance,
a fleet of which vehicles was
presented to the King by a
group of Indian Princes.
1916

David Lloyd George (in bowler hat), accompanied by General Sir Henry Mackinnon, KCB, inspecting Royal Welch Fusiliers, of the 1st Brigade of the Welsh Army Division (38th), at Llandudno on St David's Day.
1st March, 1916

A Red Cross wagon coming
from the trenches to a field
hospital at Abu Roman.
March, 1916

Crowds outside Bow Street court, for the trial of Irish separatist Roger Casement. Casement was executed for treason at Pentonville in August of that year.
April, 1916

The Gloucestershire
Regiment in Italy, marching
through Piave on the way to
the front at Asiago.
April, 1916

POBLACHT NA H EIREANN

THE PROVISIONAL GOVERNMENT
OF THE

IRISH REPUBLIC
TO THE PEOPLE OF IRELAND.

IRISHMEN AND IRISHWOMEN. In the name of God and of the dead generations from which she receives her old tradition of nationhood, Ireland, through us, summons her children to her flag and strikes for her freedom.

Having organised and trained her manhood through her secret revolutionary organisation, the Irish Republican Brotherhood, and through her open military organisations, the Irish Volunteers and the Irish Citizen Army, having patiently perfected her discipline, having resolutely waited for the right moment to reveal itself, she now seizes that moment, and, supported by her exiled children in America and by gallant allies in Europe, but relying in the first on her own strength, she strikes in full confidence of victory.

We declare the right of the people of Ireland to the ownership of Ireland, and to the unfettered control of Irish destinies, to be sovereign and indefeasible. The long usurpation of that right by a foreign people and government has not extinguished the right, nor can it ever be extinguished except by the destruction of the Irish people. In every generation the Irish people have asserted their right to national freedom and sovereignty; six times during the past three hundred years they have asserted it in arms. Standing on that fundamental right and again asserting it in arms in the face of the world, we hereby proclaim the Irish Republic as a Sovereign Independent State, and we pledge our lives and the lives of our comrades-in-arms to the cause of its freedom, of its welfare, and of its exaltation among the nations.

The Irish Republic is entitled to and hereby claims, the allegiance of every Irishman and Irishwoman. The Republic guarantees religious and civil liberty, equal rights and equal opportunities to all its citizens, and declares its resolve to pursue the happiness and prosperity of the whole nation and of all its parts, cherishing all the children of the nation equally, and oblivious of the differences carefully fostered by an alien government, which have divided a minority from the majority in the past.

Until our arms have brought the opportune moment for the establishment of a permanent National Government, representative of the whole people of Ireland and elected by the suffrages of all her men and women, the Provisional Government, hereby constituted, will administer the civil and military affairs of the Republic in trust for the people.

We place the cause of the Irish Republic under the protection of the Most High God, Whose blessing we invoke upon our arms, and we pray that no one who serves that cause will dishonour it by cowardice, inhumanity, or rapine. In this supreme hour the Irish nation must, by its valour and discipline and by the readiness of its children to sacrifice themselves for the common good, prove itself worthy of the august destiny to which it is called.

Signed on Behalf of the Provisional Government,

THOMAS J. CLARKE.
SEAN Mac DIARMADA.   THOMAS MacDONAGH.
P. H. PEARSE.   EAMONN CEANNT.
JAMES CONNOLLY.   JOSEPH PLUNKETT.

A poster issued by members of Sinn Fein proclaiming the creation of an Irish Republic. The Easter Rising in Dublin, which began on the 24th April, claimed the lives of 794 civilians and 521 soldiers and police.

24th April, 1916

Children carry wood from
Sackville Street, Dublin, after
the Easter Rising.
May, 1916

The aftermath of the Easter Rising, the ruins of the General Post Office viewed from the top of Nelson's Column, Dublin. Rebels, proclaiming an Irish Republic, seized control of the building on the 24th April.

11th May, 1916

British troops on guard
outside Cassidy's grocery
during the Easter Rising
in Dublin.
11th May, 1916

A view from Nelson's Column showing ruins in the city of Dublin after the Easter Rising. Much of the damage was caused by British artillery fire.

14th May, 1916

The Battle of Jutland, seen
from a British Destroyer.
31st May, 1916

British and French troops
with captured German guns.
June, 1916

Lady Baden Powell inspects the guard of honour of Girl Guides at Battersea Park.
June, 1916

Secretary of State for War,
David Lloyd George, talking
with Indian soldiers at the
front.
June, 1916

British 331 Infantrymen waiting to advance. More than 20,000 allied troops died on the first day of the Somme offensive.
July, 1916

The fuselage of a German aeroplane, captured in France, is paraded up Fleet Street as a trophy during the Lord Mayor's Show.
August, 1916

At the fourth attempt, Sir Ernest Shackleton succeeds in reaching Elephant Island. He made a round trip of 750 miles to South Georgia in a small boat to get help for the 22 men of his party stranded there.
30th August, 1916

The havoc wrought by the British bombardment on a German trench in front of Guillemont, near Albert, during the battle of the Somme. Guillemont was captured by the British in the same month.
September, 1916

King George V is cheered by
the crew of HMS Repulse.
Repulse saw action in both
World Wars and was sunk by
the Japanese in 1941.
1917

The Duke of Connaught
(C) and Lord Petre (L)
pay a visit to a munitions
factory. Female workers
(munitionettes) are preparing
British artillery shells
destined for the front.
1917

Queen Alexandra at Hyde
Park House Charity Sale.
1917

The Imperial War Cabinet in
the garden of 10 Downing
Street.
1917

Captain William Turner
gives evidence at
the Lusitania Inquiry.
1917

Taxi known as the 'Yellow
Bird' with lady driver.
Eastbourne, Sussex.
1917

King George V at the works
of the Clyde Shipbuilding
and Engineering Company.
1917

A woman repairs a street
lamp.
November, 1917

King George V and Queen Mary chat with a patient at a Canadian military hospital.
1918

Facing page: The wreckage of a British tank beside the infamous Menin Road near Ypres, Belgium. The Menin Road was used as a supply route by the British Army and came under intense German artillery fire.
1918

Policewomen taking part in a restraining exercise in a park in Brighton, Sussex. Women enrolled in police forces during the First World War to fill the gaps in the ranks left by the large numbers of policemen who enlisted in the Armed Forces.
1918

Women learning to drive
Walthamstow Council trams.
1918

Field Marshal Sir Douglas
Haig, with his Lancer escort,
congratulates Canadians
from the 85th Nova Scotian
Battalion after a successful
action on the Western Front.
1918

Charlie Chaplin in 'Shoulder Arms', one of the first films made by Chaplin and his brother as independents.
1918

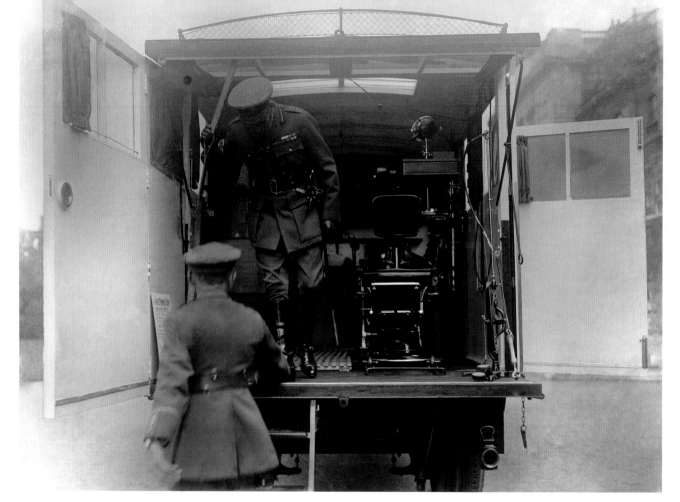

King George V inspects an
ambulance at Buckingham
Palace.
1918

Canadian troops rest in a ditch next to a newly deployed seven ton French Renault light tank.

May, 1918

Women paint the gasometer
at Cambridge Gas Works.
June, 1918

Queen Mary is presented
with a piglet during a visit
to allotments.
June, 1918

A 15 year old girl wields a cut-throat razor in a barber's shop near Waterloo Station.
14th June, 1918

King George V and Queen Mary celebrate their silver wedding at Buckingham Palace.

6th July, 1918

Massed German prisoners at a clearing station after a successful Allied offensive near Amiens in Northern France. General Ludendorff described it as 'The Black Day of the German Army'.
8th August, 1918

US President Woodrow Wilson leaves Charing Cross station in the carriage of King George V.
8th August, 1918

Royalty, servicemen and
civilians celebrate the
announcement of the
Armistice at Buckingham
Palace.
11th November, 1918

A newspaper seller displays
the Evening News headline
on Armistice day.
11th November, 1918

American troops stand
in formation in the courtyard
of Buckingham Palace.
11th November, 1918

The White Ensign flying above the Imperial German Navy flag at the surrender of the U-48 to the Royal Navy at the Essex port of Harwich. The U-48 was one of 39 U-Boats to surrender, most of them in perfect condition.

21st November, 1918

Steve Donoghue wins at Epsom on 'Lady Phoebe'.
1919

Facing page: The 'Mauretania', sister ship of the ill-fated 'Lusitania', arriving in New York with US soldiers returning from service in Europe. She still wears her wartime 'dazzle camouflage', intended to confuse U-Boats as to her position and length.
1919

Georges Clemenceau,
the French Prime Minister,
leaving Versailles after the
signing of the peace treaty.
1919

The Prince of Wales at
a Chelsea football match in
Grenadier Guards uniform.
1919

Royal Naval Unit of 12-oared
Cutters at the Thames
Pageant.
1919

Facing page: The
Whitechapel Bell Foundry
– the oldest continuous
business in the world.
1919

E Robinson (Yorkshire)
cleverly caught by P F
Warner. Middlesex v
Yorkshire – Lords.
1919

Wedding of Lieut. Duff Cooper D.S.O. – future First Lord of the Admiralty – and Lady Diana Manners, who was regarded as the most beautiful young woman in England.
1919

Charlie Chaplin and World
Welterweight Boxing
Champion Ted (Kid) Lewis.
Lewis was born Gershon
Mendeloff in Aldgate,
East London.
1919

British airship NS11 flying over the Old Bailey in London. The airship crashed with the loss of all hands off the Norfolk coast on the 15th July 1919.
1919

Charlie Hallows, Lancashire and England.
April, 1919

Facing page: Slum dwellings in London.
May, 1919

Massed choirs in Hyde Park
on Empire Day.
24th May, 1919

Facing page: The coffin of
nurse Edith Cavell, who was
executed by the German
military during the First
World War for harbouring
Allied soldiers, landing at
Dover's Promenade Pier
for reburial on Life's Green,
at the east end of Norwich
Cathedral.
May, 1919

David Lloyd George, Signor
Orlando, M. Clemenceau
and Woodrow Wilson at a
peace conference in France.
June, 1919

The Prince of Wales on his
way to the pithead on a visit
to South Wales.
June, 1919

The Royal Navy's K-3
submarine, the largest
in the world.
June, 1919

Signing of the peace treaty
by Germany and the Allies
at Versailles.
28th June, 1919

Earl Beatty leads the Navy
Peace Procession across
Westminster Bridge.
18th July, 1919

Jack Dempsey, World
Heavyweight Champion.
August, 1919

The SS Caronia, built for Cunard by John Brown & Co, arriving at Tilbury, the largest vessel ever docked in London.
3rd September, 1919

Facing page: British aviators John Alcock and Captain Arthur Whitton Brown complete the first non-stop transatlantic flight from Newfoundland to Ireland in a Vickers Vimy bomber plane; 1890 miles in just over 16 hours. Both men were subsequently knighted.
23rd August, 1919

An electric train leaving
London Bridge station during
the Great Railway Strike.
27th September, 1919

People sleeping in offices during the Great Railway Strike.
5th October, 1919

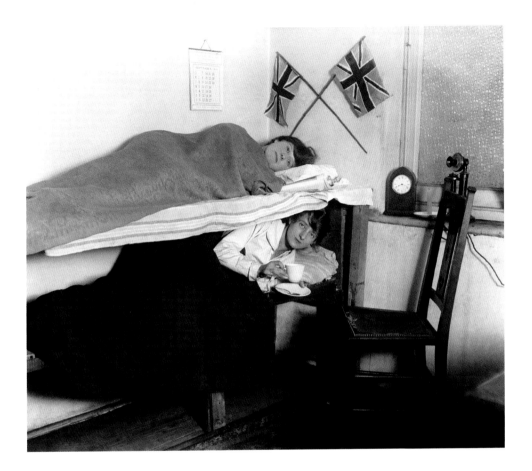

Road workers in Regent Street, London, bare their heads in a tribute to the dead on Armistice day on the anniversary of the end of the Great War.

11th November, 1919

Cavalrymen from the Scots
Greys regiment on Salisbury
Plain.
December, 1919

The Publishers gratefully acknowledge PA Photos, from whose extensive archive the photographs in this book have been selected. Personal copies of the photographs in this book, and many others, may be ordered online at www.prints.paphotos.com

For more information, please contact:

Ammonite Press

AE Publications Ltd. 166 High Street, Lewes, East Sussex, BN7 1XU, United Kingdom
Tel: 01273 488005 Fax: 01273 402866
www.ae-publications.com